40 minute
BIBLE STUDIES

Understanding
Spiritual Gifts

Kay Arthur, David & BJ Lawson

PRECEPT MINISTRIES INTERNATIONAL

WATERBROOK
PRESS

Understanding Spiritual Gifts
Published by WaterBrook Press
12265 Oracle Boulevard, Suite 200
Colorado Springs, Colorado 80921

All Scripture quotations, unless otherwise indicated, are taken from the New American Standard Bible® (NASB), © Copyright The Lockman Foundation 1960, 1962, 1963, 1968, 1971, 1972, 1973, 1975, 1977, 1995. Used by permission. (www.Lockman.org)

Italics in Scripture quotations reflect the author's added emphasis.

ISBN 978-0-307-45870-4
ISBN 978-0-307-45871-1 (electronic)

Published in the United States by WaterBrook Multnomah, an imprint of the Crown Publishing Group, a division of Random House Inc., New York.

WaterBrook and its deer colophon are registered trademarks of Random House Inc.

Printed in the United States of America
2013

10 9 8 7 6 5

Special Sales
Most WaterBrook Multnomah books are available at special quantity discounts when purchased in bulk by corporations, organizations, and special-interest groups. Custom imprinting or excerpting can also be done to fit special needs. For information, please e-mail SpecialMarkets@WaterBrookMultnomah.com or call 1-800-603-7051.

CONTENTS

HOW TO USE THIS STUDY

This small-group study is for people who are interested in learning for themselves more about what the Bible says on various subjects, but who have only limited time to meet together. It's ideal, for example, for a lunch group at work, an early morning men's group, a young mothers' group meeting in a home, a Sunday-school class, or even family devotions. (It's also ideal for small groups that typically have longer meeting times—such as evening groups or Saturday morning groups—but want to devote only a portion of their time together to actual study, while reserving the rest for prayer, fellowship, or other activities.)

This book is designed so that all the group's participants will complete each lesson's study activities *at the same time*. Discussing your insights drawn from what God says about the subject reveals exciting, life-impacting truths.

Although it's a group study, you'll need a facilitator to lead the study and keep the discussion moving. (This person's function is *not* that of a lecturer or teacher. However, when this book is used in a Sunday-school class or similar setting, the teacher should feel free to lead more directly and to bring in other insights in addition to those provided in each week's lesson.)

If *you* are your group's facilitator, the leader, here are some helpful points for making your job easier:

- Go through the lesson and mark the text before you lead the group. This will give you increased familiarity with the material and will enable you to facilitate the group with greater ease. It may be easier for you to lead the group through the instructions for marking if you, as a leader, choose a specific color for each symbol you mark.

- As you lead the group, start at the beginning of the text and simply read it aloud in the order it appears in the lesson, including the "insight boxes," which appear throughout. Work through the lesson together, observing and discussing what you learn. As you read the Scripture verses, have the group say aloud the word they are marking in the text.

- The discussion questions are there simply to help you cover the material. As the class moves into the discussion, many times you will find that they will cover the questions on their own. Remember, the discussion questions are there to guide the group through the topic, not to squelch discussion.

- Remember how important it is for people to verbalize their answers and discoveries. This greatly strengthens their personal understanding of each week's lesson. Try to ensure that everyone has plenty of opportunity to contribute to each week's discussions.

- Keep the discussion moving. This may mean spending more time on some parts of the study than on others. If necessary, you should feel free to spread out a lesson over more than one session. However, remember that you don't want to slow the pace too much. It's much better to leave everyone "wanting more" than to have people dropping out because of declining interest.

- If the validity or accuracy of some of the answers seems questionable, you can gently and cheerfully remind the group to stay focused on the truth of the Scriptures. Your object is to learn what the Bible says, not to engage in human philosophy. Simply stick with the Scriptures and give God the opportunity to speak. His Word *is* truth (John 17:17)!

UNDERSTANDING SPIRITUAL GIFTS

Many churches these days seem to place a great deal of emphasis on creating seeker-friendly environments, implementing membership growth programs, building a phenomenal multimedia ministry, and bringing on board "big-vision" staff members with charismatic personalities.

Who is really being glorified in all of this: God or man?

In our efforts to package church into something exciting, we may have overlooked one of God's key provisions for our growth and maturity: spiritual gifts.

Spiritual gifts are a necessity in the ministry of every body of believers. All of us, as Christ followers should be working together to strengthen the body, to produce unity, to be lights shining in the darkness, and to bring glory to God. This is done through the empowerment of the Holy Spirit, through the gifts that He gives us.

As the preacher A. W. Tozer wrote, "These are not natural talents merely, but gifts imparted by the Holy Spirit to fit the believer for his place in the body of Christ. They are like pipes on a great organ, permitting the musician wide scope and ranged to produce music of the finest quality. But they are, I repeat, more than talents. They are spiritual gifts."[*]

Unfortunately, many Christians seem to be unaware of the gifts of the Spirit—what they are, how they are received, or how they are to be used.

In the next six weeks of study you will learn the answers to these questions and more. As you discover a fuller vision for how God intends spiritual gifts to work within the church, your study of this subject will prepare you to tap into God's agenda and play an active role in His ministry, not only to the body of Christ but possibly even to the rest of the world.

> We have yet to see what God would do for His Church if we would all throw ourselves down before Him with an open Bible and cry, "Behold Thy servant, Lord! Be it unto me even as Thou wilt!"[†]

---

[*] A.W. Tozer, *Keys to the Deeper Life* (Grand Rapids: Zondervan, 1984), 44.
[†] Tozer, *Keys to the Deeper Life*, 47

Sometimes the subject of spiritual gifts seems so confusing it can be hard to even know where to start the discussion. There are so many questions. Who has a spiritual gift? All of us? Or are they for super-spiritual people only?

To get the answers, we're going to go straight to the gift giver Himself and let Him explain the gifts. As you read for yourself the straightforward truths of the Bible, we believe you'll find the subject is not nearly as complicated a subject as you may have thought.

First, we'll consider these two questions: what kind of gifts are there, and who qualifies to receive one?

OBSERVE

Jesus prepared Peter for the world's tribulation; then Peter was to prepare others. So the apostle wrote a letter to the "chosen," the believers scattered throughout Asia during the intense persecution of their day, to encourage them and instruct them in how to live according to God's will (1 Peter 1:2; 4:2).

Leader: Read 1 Peter 4:10–11 aloud. Have the group say aloud and...

- *draw a box around each reference to **a gift**, including the pronoun **it**:* ☐
- *underline the phrase **each one,** which refers here to **believers**.*

1 PETER 4:10–11

¹⁰As each one has received a special gift, employ it in serving one another as good stewards of the manifold grace of God.

¹¹ Whoever speaks, is to do so as one who is speaking the utterances of God; whoever serves is to do so as one who is serving by the strength which

God supplies; so that in all things God may be glorified through Jesus Christ, to whom belongs the glory and dominion forever and ever. Amen.

As you read the text, it's helpful to have the group say the key words aloud as they mark them. This way everyone will be sure they are marking every occurrence of the word, including any synonymous words or phrases. Do this throughout the study.

INSIGHT

One way to better understand what the text is saying is by asking the "5 Ws and an H" questions—*who, what, when, where, why,* and *how*—about the passage. By asking these questions, you slow down and actually see what the writer is saying.

DISCUSS

• **Who** receives a gift?

• **What** is this passage about?

• **What** are believers to do with the gift they have been given?

• **How** are they to use what they've received?

• Is the gift to be used for one's personal benefit? Explain your answer.

INSIGHT

A *spiritual gift* is a God-given ability to serve God and other Christians in such a way that Christ is glorified and believers are edified. Each believer has at least one spiritual gift, no matter what his or her natural abilities.

• **What** two categories did Peter divide the gifts into?   *Speaking*
    Serving

• **What** are those who speak supposed to speak?   *Speak as one who is speaking the utterance of God*

• **How** are those who serve to carry out their role?   *Do to be one who is serving by the strength which God supplies*

• **Why** are we to use our gifts in the way described? Look carefully at the end of verse 11 if you need a hint. *So that Jesus Christ may be glorified*

• Now let's evaluate what you just read and see how it applies to you. Looking at your experience serving in the church and your desire to do so, which category better describes the way God has equipped you: serving or speaking?

• What have others said to you that confirms this?

Acts 6:1–6

¹ Now at this time while the disciples were increasing in number, a complaint arose on the part of the Hellenistic Jews against the native Hebrews, because their widows were being overlooked in the daily serving of food.

OBSERVE

The early church experienced growing pains that alerted the disciples to the impossibility of doing all the work themselves.

Leader: Read Acts 6:1–6 aloud. Have the group…
  • *circle the words* **serving** *and* **serve.**
  • *draw a box around each reference to **the word.***

DISCUSS

- What complaint had arisen within the congregation? *Widows were being overlooked in the daily serving of food*

- How did the twelve respond, according to verse 2? What does this tell you about their understanding of their gifts? *They did not want to neglect the word of God in order to serve tables*

- What type of gifts did the twelve have? *Speaking*

- What category of gifts was needed to resolve the conflict? *Service*

- Many people today believe the pastoral staff should take care of all the work related to the life of the church. From what you saw in this passage, is this true? Explain your answer. *No it isn't true. Those who cannot teach the word should serve.*

2 So the twelve summoned the congregation of the disciples and said, "It is not desirable for us to neglect the word of God in order to serve tables.

3 "Therefore, brethren, select from among you seven men of good reputation, full of the Spirit and of wisdom, whom we may put in charge of this task.

4 "But we will devote ourselves to prayer and to the ministry of the word."

5 The statement found approval with the whole congregation; and they chose Stephen, a man full of faith and of the Holy Spirit, and Philip, Prochorus,

Nicanor, Timon, Parmenas and Nicolas, a proselyte from Antioch.

6 And these they brought before the apostles; and after praying, they laid their hands on them.

EPHESIANS 4:1–6

1 Therefore I, the prisoner of the Lord, implore you to walk in a manner worthy of the calling with which you have been called,

2 with all humility and gentleness, with patience, showing tolerance for one another in love,

3 being diligent to preserve the unity of the Spirit in the bond of peace.

• How does this relate to what you read in 1 Peter?

Some are gifted to teach the word. Others should serve

OBSERVE

In the first three chapters of his letter to the Ephesians, Paul described the awesome reality of our salvation. In chapter 3 he specifically wrote about the fact that faith in Christ brings unity to radically different people groups, such as the Jews and the Gentiles. Writing in light of these things, he opened with the word *therefore* in Ephesians 4:1.

Leader: Read Ephesians 4:1–6 aloud. Have the group say and …

• *mark references to **unity,** including the word **one,** with a semicircle, like this:*

⌒

• *draw a stick figure over the word **body,** like this:* ⚲

DISCUSS

• List the behaviors and characteristics Paul instructed the believers to display in verses 1–2. *walk in a manner worthy of your calling humility gentleness patience tolerance in love*

• According to verse 3, why are we to behave this way? *to preserve unity of the Spirit*

• What did you learn from marking *one* in verses 4–6?

• How does this apply to our discussion of spiritual gifts? *One body different gifts*

4 There is one body and one Spirit, just as also you were called in one hope of your calling;

5 one Lord, one faith, one baptism,

6 one God and Father of all who is over all and through all and in all.

EPHESIANS 4:7–8, 11–16

7 But to each one of us grace was given according to the measure of Christ's gift.

8 Therefore it says, "When He [Jesus] ascended on high, He led captive a host of captives, and He gave gifts to men."…

11 And He gave some as apostles, and some as prophets, and some as evangelists, and some as pastors and teachers,

12 for the equipping of the saints for the work of service, to the building up of the body of Christ;

13 until we all attain to the unity of the faith, and of the

OBSERVE

Paul moved from describing what all believers have in common to detailing how they differ from one another. Let's look at what he identified as areas of individuality within the unity of the Spirit.

Leader: *Read Ephesians 4:7–8 and 11–16 aloud. Have the group say and…*
  - *draw a box around the words **given, gave,** and **gifts.***
  - *mark every reference to **the body** with a stick figure.*

Leader: *Read the passage again. This time have the group…*
  - *say aloud and mark each reference to **Christ,** including synonyms and pronouns, with a cross:* ✝

DISCUSS

- According to verses 7 and 8, who gave what to whom?

• When did this happen?

• Make a list of the gifts mentioned in verse 11.

INSIGHT

Apostle—one sent forth with a message.

Prophet—one with the God-given ability to speak forth a message from God's Word that edifies, exhorts, and/or comforts the body.

Evangelist—a messenger of the good news; one who shares the gospel clearly that others may come to faith in Jesus.

Pastors and teachers care for and teach local congregations.

  Pastor—a shepherd; one who feeds, tends, protects the flock

  Teacher—an instructor who teaches the truth of the Word in a clear and understandable way

---

knowledge of the Son of God, to a mature man, to the measure of the stature which belongs to the fullness of Christ.

14 As a result, we are no longer to be children, tossed here and there by waves and carried about by every wind of doctrine, by the trickery of men, by craftiness in deceitful scheming;

15 but speaking the truth in love, we are to grow up in all aspects into Him who is the head, even Christ,

16 from whom the whole body, being fitted and held together by what every joint supplies, according to

the proper working of each individual part, causes the growth of the body for the building up of itself in love.

• Were all of the gifts given to everyone? Explain your answer.

• Which category of gifts would these fit into: speaking or serving?

• What is the purpose of these gifts, according to verse 12? *Equipping of the saints*

• How long are the gifts needed?
Until we all attain the unity of the faith and the knowledge of the Son of God

• Ultimately, what are we to look like as we walk in the gifts we have received?
Jesus

• According to verse 16, how are these gifts tied to the health of the church?

WRAP IT UP

While we will spend the next five weeks studying the topic of spiritual gifts in greater depth, the simple truth from this week's lesson is that you are gifted by God.

As we've clearly seen, "each one has received a *special* gift…" (1 Peter 4:10). This means that, if you are a follower of Christ, then you have been gifted by God to serve the body of Christ, the church.

That knowledge should be a tremendous encouragement to you. What an incredible privilege!

We also saw this week that, broadly speaking, the spiritual gifts given to believers fall into two categories: serving and speaking. Neither category is more important than the other, because all the gifts are intended to equip the saints and build up the body. Every gift is important.

If you don't already know what your spiritual gift is, spend some time this week reflecting on the ways you're already involved in meeting the needs of others or in fulfilling a particular role within the church. Most people are naturally drawn to areas of ministry that fit their gifting, so this may help give you some insight.

If you're *not* actively involved in your church in some way, we encourage you to consider why that is. If you are follower of Christ, He has equipped you and called you to take an active role in His work. Will you prove worthy of His calling?

We learned last week that spiritual gifts fall into two general categories: speaking and serving. But where do these gifts come from and when did this expression of the Holy Spirit start? What can a person do to acquire these gifts?

This week we will answer these questions and continue to look at the purpose of spiritual gifts.

OBSERVE

Acts 1:9 records Jesus' ascension, an event mentioned in Ephesians 4:8, which we looked at last week. In writing the book of Acts, Luke focused his attention on the fulfillment of Jesus' promise of the coming of the Holy Spirit and the power the disciples would receive at the Spirit's arrival. This event marked the beginning of the church. The role of the Holy Spirit in the growth and development of the young Christian church is a theme throughout the book of Acts.

In the passage we're about to read, the word *they* in verse 1 refers to the disciples.

ACTS 2:1–13

1 When the day of Pentecost had come, they were all together in one place.

2 And suddenly there came from heaven a noise like a violent rushing wind, and it filled the whole house where they were sitting.

3 And there appeared to them tongues as of fire distributing themselves, and they rested on each one of them.

4 And they were all filled with the Holy Spirit and began to speak with other tongues, as the Spirit was giving them utterance.

5 Now there were Jews living in Jerusalem, devout men from every nation under heaven.

6 And when this sound occurred, the crowd came together, and were bewildered because each one of them was hearing them speak in his own language.

7 They were amazed and astonished, saying, "Why, are not all these who are speaking Galileans?

Leader: Read Acts 2:1–13 aloud. Have the group do the following:

- *draw a cloud shape like this* ⌒⌒⌒ *around each mention of the Holy Spirit or the Spirit.*
- *mark a big* **D** *over each occurrence of the pronouns **they, themselves,** and **them,** which refer to **the disciples** in this passage.*
- *underline each occurrence of the words **speak, speaking,** and **utterance.***

DISCUSS

- Keeping in mind the "five Ws and an H," discuss the events described in this passage.

- **When** did this take place?

- **What** happened in verses 2–4, when they were all together?

• **How** does this relate to what we saw last week in Ephesians 4:8?

• **Who** was present when this happened? In other words, what groups of people witnessed the event?

• **How** did they hear the disciples' message, according to verse 11? **What** did they hear?

• **What** was the response of these witnesses?

• **What** were they asking in verse 12?

8 "And how is it that we each hear them in our own language to which we were born?

9 "Parthians and Medes and Elamites, and residents of Mesopotamia, Judea and Cappadocia, Pontus and Asia,

10 Phrygia and Pamphylia, Egypt and the districts of Libya around Cyrene, and visitors from Rome, both Jews and proselytes,

11 Cretans and Arabs—we hear them in our own tongues speaking of the mighty deeds of God."

12 And they all continued in amazement and great perplexity,

saying to one another, "What does this mean?"

13 But others were mocking and saying, "They are full of sweet wine."

• The word *but* in verse 13 indicates a contrast. What is the contrast?

ACTS 2:14–21

14 But Peter, taking his stand with the eleven, raised his voice and declared to them: "Men of Judea and all you who live in Jerusalem, let this be known to you and give heed to my words.

15 "For these men are not drunk, as you suppose, for it is only the third hour of the day;

16 but this is what was spoken of through the prophet Joel:

OBSERVE

In response to the confusion of the crowd, Peter explained that they were witnessing the fulfillment of an Old Testament prophecy.

Leader: Read Acts 2:14–21 aloud. Have the group do the following:
- *mark every reference to **Peter,** including pronouns, with a big **P.***
- *draw a cloud around each occurrence of the phrase **My Spirit.***
- *underline **this is what was spoken of through the prophet Joel.***

DISCUSS

• What kinds of gifts were evident as Peter responded to the Jews in Jerusalem? Were they speaking gifts or serving gifts?

• How did Peter respond to the accusation that these men were drunk?

• According to verse 18, what was happening?

• What is the proof of the Holy Spirit's presence in this passage?

• Who was Peter quoting?

17 'And it shall be in the last days,' God says, 'That I will pour forth of My Spirit on all mankind; and your sons and your daughters shall prophesy, and your young men shall see visions, and your old men shall dream dreams;

18 Even on My bond-slaves, both men and women, I will in those days pour forth of My Spirit and they shall prophesy.

19 'And I will grant wonders in the sky above and signs on the earth below, blood, and fire, and vapor of smoke.

20 'The sun will be turned into darkness and the moon into blood, before the great and glorious day of the Lord shall come.

21 'And it shall be that everyone who calls on the name of the Lord will be saved.' "

EPHESIANS 4:8

Therefore it says, "When He ascended on high, He led captive a host of captives, and He gave gifts to men."

• Keeping in mind the two categories of gifts we saw last week, what category does Peter's gift fall into: serving or speaking?

OBSERVE

By way of reminder, let's look at Ephesians 4:8 again. The *He* mentioned here refers to Jesus.

Leader: Read Ephesians 4:8 aloud.
   • *Have the group say aloud and draw a box around the word **gifts**.*

DISCUSS

• What did Jesus give to men?

• When did He do it?

OBSERVE

Joel had prophesied that one day the Spirit would come. Jesus Himself had promised to fulfill the prophecy by sending the gift of the Holy Spirit to His people.

Leader: Read John 16:7 and Acts 2:33 aloud. Have the group say and…
- *mark with a cross the pronouns **I** and **He**, which refer to **Jesus** in these verses.*
- *draw a cloud around every reference to **the Holy Spirit,** including the synonym **Helper** and the pronoun **Him.***

DISCUSS

- What did you learn from marking the references to Jesus?

- What did you learn from marking references to the Holy Spirit?

JOHN 16:7

But I tell you the truth, it is to your advantage that I go away; for if I do not go away, the Helper will not come to you; but if I go, I will send Him to you.

ACTS 2:33

Therefore having been exalted to the right hand of God, and having received from the Father the promise of the Holy Spirit, He has poured forth this which you both see and hear.

Acts 2:37–43

37 Now when they heard this, they were pierced to the heart, and said to Peter and the rest of the apostles, "Brethren, what shall we do?"

38 Peter said to them, "Repent, and each of you be baptized in the name of Jesus Christ for the forgiveness of your sins; and you will receive the gift of the Holy Spirit.

39 "For the promise is for you and your children and for all who are far off, as many as the Lord our God will call to Himself."

40 And with many other words he solemnly testified and

OBSERVE

The Holy Spirit used Peter's sermon to convict those listening of their part in Christ's death.

Leader: Read Acts 2:37–43 aloud. Have the group …
- *mark **Holy Spirit** with a cloud.*
- *underline the phrases **with many other words** and **his words.***

DISCUSS

- What question did those listening ask Peter when they recognized their sin?

- How did Peter respond?

• What action(s) did Peter link to the gift of the Holy Spirit?

• Last week we looked at the following gifts: apostles, prophets, evangelists, pastors and teachers. Peter was an apostle; what other gift or gifts do we see in him?

• Are these speaking gifts or serving gifts?

kept on exhorting them, saying, "Be saved from this perverse generation!"

41 So then, those who had received his word were baptized; and that day there were added about three thousand souls.

42 They were continually devoting themselves to the apostles' teaching and to fellowship, to the breaking of bread and to prayer.

43 Everyone kept feeling a sense of awe; and many wonders and signs were taking place through the apostles.

WRAP IT UP

The gift of the Holy Spirit was given initially by God at the feast called Pentecost. The Holy Spirit was poured out on the disciples of Jesus, and their lives were radically changed. They could not help themselves. They were overcome by the power and presence of the Lord. As a result they proclaimed the "mighty deeds of God" (Acts 2:11).

The first outpouring of the Spirit and the first expression of the gifts He gives centered on proclaiming the excellencies of God. The focus of the gift was God. This is vital to keep in mind as we explore the topic of spiritual gifts and their purpose. One mistake some Christians make is turning the focus of spiritual gifts toward ourselves. We get excited about *our* gift and the ways *we* can exercise it, forgetting that the gift is a working of the Holy Spirit in our lives for the purpose of bringing glory to God.

Are you using your gifting to glorify God? Are you always seeking to be sure that God is glorified by your life and your ministry, or are you drawing attention to yourself? Sometimes it's inevitable that we receive some attention as we serve, but we should always seek to redirect that attention to God.

Take a few minutes and examine the ways you seek to make a difference in your local church and elsewhere. Who is getting the glory?

The believers at Corinth were not really all that different from believers today. They had a lot of questions about spiritual gifts and how the gifts were to operate in the church. Paul's answers to them serve as clear instructions to us, so that's where we'll focus much of our study this week.

OBSERVE

Leader: Read 1 Corinthians 12:1 aloud.

- *Have the group say aloud and draw a box around the word* **gifts**.

1 CORINTHIANS 12:1

Now concerning spiritual gifts, brethren, I do not want you to be unaware.

DISCUSS

• What was Paul's concern in this verse?

That his congregation not be unaware

OBSERVE

Leader: Read 1 Corinthians 12:4–7 aloud. Have the group say and...

- *circle each occurrence of the word* **varieties**.
- *draw a box around the word* **gifts**.
- *underline the phrase* **each one.**

1 CORINTHIANS 12:4–7

⁴ Now there are varieties of gifts, but the same Spirit.

⁵ And there are varieties of ministries, and the same Lord.

6 There are varieties of effects, but the same God who works all things in all persons.

7 But to each one is given the manifestation of the Spirit for the common good.

DISCUSS

• Three times we see the phrase *there are varieties of.* What are these three things that come in different varieties?

INSIGHT

The Greek word used in this passage for *gifts* is *charisma,* which means "a gift of grace, a spiritual endowment."

• According to verse 4 are all gifts the same?

No — a variety

• Will everyone have the same gift?

No

• Are the gifts earned or achieved, according to verse 7? Explain your answer.

No. They are given

• Who gives the gifts and for what purpose?

God for God's Glory (It is)

• According to verse 5, will everyone have the same ministry?

No

• Who gives or directs these ministries?

God

• Will everyone have the same results?

No

• According to verse 6, who is responsible for the ministry results?

God

• How would your approach to ministry be affected by knowing who determines the results?

- Verse 7 begins with the word but, which shows a contrast is being made. How does verse 7 relate to verse 6?

  but all are given the manifestation.

- Who is given a spiritual gift, according to verse 7? *all*

- How does verse 7 define a spiritual gift?

  manifestation of the Spirit

ACTS 20:24

But I do not consider my life of any account as dear to myself, so that I may finish my course and the ministry which I received from the Lord Jesus, to testify solemnly of the gospel of the grace of God.

OBSERVE

At one point in his ministry, Paul noted that the Holy Spirit warned him that "bonds and afflictions" lay ahead. Let's see what compelled him to continue on despite the danger.

Leader: Read Acts 20:24 aloud.
- *Have the group say and mark the word* **ministry** *with a big* **M.**

DISCUSS

- Where did Paul say his ministry came from?

• What did he say his ministry was?

To testify solemly ~~*B*~~ *the gospel*
of the grace of God

• How does this compare to what you saw
in 1 Corinthians 12:5?

There are various ministries.
Testifying solemly was Pauls

OBSERVE

Let's return to 1 Corinthians 12, where
Paul continued talking to believers who are
given different gifts, have different ministries, and through whom God is still
working different effects. The word *for* in
verse 8 makes clear that what follows is a
further explanation of the preceding verses,
1 Corinthians 12:1–7.

Leader: Read 1 Corinthians 12:8–11 aloud.
Have the group…

   • *double underline the phrases **to one, to***
     ***another**, and **to each one**.*

   • *draw a cloud around each reference to*
     the Spirit: ☁

Leader: Read 1 Corinthians 12:8–11 again.

   • *This time number each of **the spiritual***
     ***gifts** listed. We have numbered the first*
     two for you.

1 CORINTHIANS 12:8–11

8 For to one is given
the word of ①wisdom
through the Spirit,
and to another the
word of ②knowledge
according to the same
Spirit;

9 to another faith
by the same Spirit,
and to another gifts
of healing by the one
Spirit,

10 and to another
the effecting of
miracles, and to
another prophecy,
and to another the
distinguishing of
spirits, to another

various kinds of tongues, and to another the [9] interpretation of tongues.

[11] But one and the same Spirit works all these things, distributing to each one individually just as He wills.

DISCUSS

• List the nine gifts noted in this passage.

word of wisdom
word of knowledge
faith   *prophecy*
healing *distinguishing spirits*
miracles *tongues (interp of tongues*

• Are all believers given the same gift?

No

• What did you learn from marking references to the Spirit?

• According to verse 11 how does He distribute the gifts?

just as He wills

• What happens when someone tries to be just like someone else in gifting and ministry?

• Can you ask for or earn certain gifts? Explain your answer.

INSIGHT

Word of wisdom—a clear insight into the true nature of things so that application can be made from that clear insight.

Word of knowledge—a seeking to know, investigation, an inquiry of God's revelation and truth; communication of knowledge.

Faith—an unusual measure of trust in God. This is not the faith all must have for salvation; this is mountain-moving faith, faith that believes God, trusts God when others can't.

Gifts of healings—ability to restore health.

Effectings of miracles—workings of supernatural acts that can only be explained as being of God.

Prophecy—ability to speak forth a message from God's Word that edifies, exhorts, and/or comforts the body.

Distinguishing of spirits—the supernatural ability to distinguish between truth and error, between people of God or the devil

Kinds of tongues—supernatural ability to speak an unlearned known language

Interpretation of tongues—a supernatural ability to translate an unlearned known language

1 Corinthians 12:28–31

28 And God has appointed in the church, first apostles, second prophets, third teachers, then miracles, then gifts of healings, helps, administrations, various kinds of tongues.

29 All are not apostles, are they? All are not prophets, are they? All are not teachers, are they? All are not workers of miracles, are they?

30 All do not have gifts of healings, do they? All do not speak with tongues, do they? All do not interpret, do they?

31 But earnestly desire the greater gifts. And I show you a still more excellent way.

OBSERVE

Leader: Read 1 Corinthians 12:28–31 aloud.

- *Have the group say aloud and mark each occurrence of the word **all** with a big **A**.*

DISCUSS

- List what God has appointed in the church. apostles administrations prophets teachers tongues miracles healings helps

- How would you respond to someone who was teaching that we must all have the same gifts or that a particular gift must be present in one's life as a sign of true faith?

- From what you have seen, who is responsible to assign spiritual gifts? Holy Spirit

• Does verse 31 contradict what Paul has been teaching up to this point? Explain your answer.

No, He is about to explain how doing whatever one does through love is better than desiring greater gifts

• What have you learned this week about spiritual gifts?

• As you consider the gifts you saw described in this lesson, do you believe any are present in your own life? Explain what evidence leads you to that conclusion.

WRAP IT UP

The implications of this week's study are truly freeing. The Holy Spirit gives the gifts as He wills. We are not responsible to earn them, nor are we invited to pick and choose our favorite. There is no need to worry about whether or not we have the right one, the best one. The Holy Spirit in His sovereign will assigned us our gift, or gifts, at His discretion so that each one of us can fulfill God's unique purpose for our lives.

The Lord Jesus Christ gives us ministries as He wills. We are not responsible to find our own and hope we have the right one, the best one. It is completely up to Him. We receive our appointed ministry at His discretion; we do not achieve a ministry by our own work or skill. The Lord assigns each ministry, and we receive it from His hand. We are not even responsible for the results! It is God who accomplishes His purpose through us and determines the outcome of our ministry efforts.

The creator God does not need us at all, but in His grace and mercy He chooses to use us to accomplish ministry in His church. In a sense He allows us through our gifts and our ministries to become co-laborers with Him in this world. What amazing grace!

We are not to seek "greater" gifts; we seek the gift giver.

We are not to seek the greater ministries; we seek the minister of ministries, our Lord Jesus Christ.

We are not even to seek after great results; we seek to give glory to the One who provides the results.

Pursue hard after God. He will show you your gift, your place of service, and He will even provide the results. So seek your joy in God; He will accomplish the rest.

It surprises some people to discover that spiritual gifts—a distinctly New Testament phenomenon that manifests the presence of the Holy Spirit—are only discussed in four different passages in the Bible. This week we will look at Paul's teaching on gifts in his letter to the church in Rome.

OBSERVE

Paul's letter to the Romans is divided into two sections: chapters 1–11 tell us what God has done to bring about salvation, and chapters 12–16 show how we are to live once we have experienced salvation. Let's look at the first two verses of chapter 12, which provide the transition from the doctrinal passages into the section on practical living.

Leader: Read Romans 12:1–2 aloud.
  • *Have the group say aloud and circle each occurrence of the words* **brethren,** **you,** *and* **your.**

DISCUSS

• To whom was Paul speaking?

ROMANS 12:1–2

1 Therefore I urge you, brethren, by the mercies of God, to present your bodies a living and holy sacrifice, acceptable to God, which is your spiritual service of worship.

2 And do not be conformed to this world, but be transformed by the renewing of your mind, so that you may prove what the will of God is, that which is good and acceptable and perfect.

• What are believers called to do?

• How are we to do that, and what is to be our motivation?

• In verse 2 the will of God is described as "good and acceptable and perfect." What did Paul say is required for one to discern, or be sure of, the will of God?

• How might this relate to spiritual gifts?

ROMANS 12:3–8

3 For through the grace given to me I say to everyone among you not to think more highly of himself than he ought to think; but to think so as to have sound judgment, as God has allotted to each a measure of faith.

4 For just as we have many members in one

OBSERVE

Leader: Read Romans 12:3–8 aloud. Have the group...

• *draw a box around the words **given** and **gifts**.*
• *number each **gift** listed in the text.*

DISCUSS

• Do all believers have the same gifts?

INSIGHT

Service—to attend to, serve, aid, minister to

Teaching—to instruct, teach the truth of the Word in a clear and understandable way

Exhortation—the God-given ability to encourage, motivate, to give strength and assurance, and to offer comfort and hope

Giving—to give over, share; impart

Leadership—the God-given ability to call and to lead others so that they follow the Lord.

Mercy—to demonstrate compassion; to feel sympathy with the misery of another, especially sympathy manifested in action; to extend help

• What do verses 6–8 say about spiritual gifts and how each is to be used?

body and all the members do not have the same function,

5 so we, who are many, are one body in Christ, and individually members one of another.

6 Since we have gifts that differ according to the grace given to us, each of us is to exercise them accordingly: if prophecy, according to the proportion of his faith;

7 if service, in his serving; or he who teaches, in his teaching;

8 or he who exhorts, in his exhortation; he who gives, with liberality; he who leads, with diligence; he who shows mercy, with cheerfulness.

- Is it enough to know what your gifts are? Explain your answer.

- If your ministry is dictated by your gifts and God directs the area of service, should you feel pride in your ministry or gifting? Explain your answer.

- How would identifying your spiritual gift(s) enable you to more effectively serve your church?

- Do you believe you have any of the gifts mentioned in this passage? If so, which one(s) and why?

- Have you ever tried to serve outside your area of giftedness? If so, what happened? Share your story with the group.

• Before we leave Romans 12, let us just ask, have you submitted yourself to the Lord by presenting yourself as a living sacrifice?

OBSERVE

We studied this next passage in an earlier lesson. However, let's take another look to see which specific gifts are evident.

Leader: Read Acts 6:1–6 aloud. Have the group...
- *mark **serving** and **serve** with a big **S**.*
- *draw a squiggly line under the phrases **word of God** and **ministry of the word**, like this:* ∿∿∿∿

DISCUSS

• We have seen that gifts can be divided into two broad categories: speaking and serving. How do you see these categories exhibited in this passage?

Acts 6:1–6

1 Now at this time while the disciples were increasing in number, a complaint arose on the part of the Hellenistic Jews against the native Hebrews, because their widows were being overlooked in the daily serving of food.

2 So the twelve summoned the congregation of the disciples and said, "It is not desirable for us to neglect the word of God in order to serve tables.

3 "Therefore, brethren, select from

among you seven men of good reputation, full of the Spirit and of wisdom, whom we may put in charge of this task.

4 "But we will devote ourselves to prayer and to the ministry of the word."

5 The statement found approval with the whole congregation; and they chose Stephen, a man full of faith and of the Holy Spirit, and Philip, Prochorus, Nicanor, Timon, Parmenas and Nicolas, a proselyte from Antioch.

6 And these they brought before the apostles; and after praying, they laid their hands on them.

• What gifts seem to be evident in this passage?

OBSERVE

Let's spend the rest of our time this week looking at an example from Scripture of one of the gifts in action.

Leader: Read Acts 4:36–37 aloud.
- *Have the group say aloud and mark each reference to **Barnabas,** including the name **Joseph** and the pronoun **who**, with a big **B.***

DISCUSS

- What was the meaning of the nickname the apostles gave Joseph?

- What spiritual gift or gifts do you think Barnabas had? Explain your answer.

ACTS 4:36–37

36 Now Joseph, a Levite of Cyprian birth, who was also called Barnabas by the apostles (which translated means Son of Encouragement),

37 and who owned a tract of land, sold it and brought the money and laid it at the apostles' feet.

ACTS 9:22, 26–28

22 But Saul kept increasing in strength and confounding the Jews who lived at Damascus by proving that this Jesus is the Christ....

26 When he came to Jerusalem, he was trying to associate with the disciples; but they were all afraid of him, not believing that he was a disciple.

27 But Barnabas took hold of him and brought him to the apostles and described to them how he had seen the Lord on the road, and that He had talked to him, and how at Damascus he had spoken out boldly in the name of Jesus.

OBSERVE

The man named Saul in this next passage later became known by his Greek name, Paul, the apostle.

Leader: Read Acts 9:22, 26–28 aloud.
   • *Have the group say and mark **Barnabas** with a **B**.*

DISCUSS

• Discuss how Barnabas exercised a gift of exhortation in this passage. (If necessary, look back at page 39 for a reminder of what it means to exhort.)

• What difference did Barnabas make in the life and ministry of Paul by putting his spiritual gift into practice?

OBSERVE

Leader: Read Acts 15:36–39 aloud.
   • *Have the group say and mark* **Barnabas** *with a* **B.**

DISCUSS

• How did Barnabas exercise the gift of exhortation in this passage?

• What difference do you imagine the encouragement from Barnabas would have made in Mark's life?

---

28 And he was with them, moving about freely in Jerusalem, speaking out boldly in the name of the Lord.

Acts 15:36–39

36 After some days Paul said to Barnabas, "Let us return and visit the brethren in every city in which we proclaimed the word of the Lord, and see how they are."

37 Barnabas wanted to take John, called Mark, along with them also.

38 But Paul kept insisting that they should not take him along who had deserted them in Pamphylia and had not gone with them to the work.

39 And there occurred such a sharp disagreement that they separated from one another, and Barnabas took Mark with him and sailed away to Cyprus.

• How have you seen this gift put to work by someone in your church or ministry? Share an example with the group.

WRAP IT UP

It is no accident that in Paul's letter to the Romans the discussion of spiritual gifts follows the call to present our bodies as a living sacrifice. That act of surrender provides the basis for understanding God's good and acceptable and perfect will for how we are to carry out our giftedness and purpose in the body of Christ. Unless we are totally surrendered to the will of God, we will never be effective in carrying out the work He has planned for us.

Are you wondering how God has gifted you for ministry in the body of Christ? The first step is total surrender to His will and death to your own. God normally reveals His will when we have already committed to obey it. When you say to the Lord, "Whatever you have called me to do or be, Your will be done in my life," it is then, at the moment of surrender, that He moves to reveal His gift in you, and His ministry through you.

When you have surrendered your life as a "spiritual service of worship" (Romans 12:1), you are not swayed off course by the opinions or criticisms of others. Barnabas serves as a powerful example of faithful perseverance in the face of opposition. When the other believers refused to accept Paul after he declared his faith in Jesus, Barnabas came alongside him and stood with Paul against popular opinion. Later, when Paul became upset with John Mark and wanted to leave him behind, Barnabas stood with the young disciple against his old friend Paul. It is clear he exercised his gift in surrender to God, not subject to the influence of others.

What about you, friend? Are you seeking to exercise your spiritual gift in your way and your time? If so, you will never be effective. The first step is accepting the will of God for your life, and then walking in the gift and ministry He reveals. The results you'll see will come directly from Him.

Have you presented your body as a living sacrifice?

How can people with different personalities, backgrounds, and gifts worship together? How can they minister together? How is it possible that people from all walks of life and from various socioeconomic backgrounds can fit together in a way that it seems natural, even normal? The answer is found in the way God designed the body of Christ, the church, to operate.

This week we will look at one of the most amazing aspects of how spiritual gifts function.

OBSERVE

In week 3 we looked at the first part of 1 Corinthians 12 and learned about the variety of gifts, ministries, and effects each believer is given by God, "just as He wills" (verse 11). Let's look now at Paul's explanation of the divine design at work through this variety.

Leader: Read 1 Corinthians 12:12–13 aloud. Have the group say aloud and...
- *draw a stick figure over each occurrence of the word **body**, like this:* ☺
- *circle every reference to **members**, including pronouns.*

1 CORINTHIANS 12:12–13

12 For even as the body is one and yet has many members, and all the members of the body, though they are many, are one body, so also is Christ.

13 For by one Spirit we were all baptized into one body, whether Jews or Greeks, whether slaves or free, and we were all made to drink of one Spirit.

DISCUSS

• Discuss what you learned from marking *body.*

• In what way are believers like parts of a body, from what you read here?

INSIGHT

The baptism of the Spirit mentioned in 1 Corinthians 12:13 is experienced by all who believe, at the moment of salvation (Romans 8:9–11). This baptism identifies us with Christ. Now, regardless of our nationality (Jews or Greeks) or position in life (slave or free), we are part of one body and filled with the Holy Spirit.

• How does this relate to what you have seen in regard to believers and spiritual gifts?

OBSERVE

Leader: Read 1 Corinthians 12:14–18 *aloud. Have the group…*

- *draw a stick figure over each occurrence of the word* **body.**
- *circle the words* **member(s)** *and* **many.**

DISCUSS

- What did you learn about the body?

- What did you learn about the function of each member?

- How important is each member of the body?

- Who placed the members in the body? What determined how they were placed?

1 CORINTHIANS 12:14–18

14 For the body is not one member, but many.

15 If the foot says, "Because I am not a hand, I am not a part of the body," it is not for this reason any the less a part of the body.

16 And if the ear says, "Because I am not an eye, I am not a part of the body," it is not for this reason any the less a part of the body.

17 If the whole body were an eye, where would the hearing be? If the whole were hearing, where would the sense of smell be?

18 But now God has placed the members, each one of them, in the body, just as He desired.

• Should a believer think of himself or his gift as inferior? Why or why not?

• Should he desire another member's gift or wish he had a different gift? Explain your answer.

---

1 CORINTHIANS 12:19–24A

19 If they were all one member, where would the body be?

20 But now there are many members, but one body.

21 And the eye cannot say to the hand, "I have no need of you"; or again the head to the feet, "I have no need of you."

22 On the contrary, it is much truer that the members of the body

OBSERVE

Leader: *Read 1 Corinthians 12:19–24a aloud. Have the group…*
- *circle each reference to **member(s).***
- *draw a stick figure over every occurrence of the word **body.***

DISCUSS

• What did you learn about the members of the body?

• Is one particular member more important than another? Explain your answer.

• Discuss the relationship each member has with the others. Are they in competition with one another?

- Think about the human body. What happens to the body when its members work together? When they work independently?

- How does that relate to the church?

- Can a hand alone constitute an entire body? Have you ever tried to smell through your ears? Discuss how God's design plays out in the use of body parts.

- Does your spiritual gift change when a need arises? What does your answer suggest about God's intent for the body of Christ?

- From all you have seen, are speaking gifts any more important than serving gifts?

- What do verses 22–24 reveal about how God wants us to view "weaker" members?

which seem to be weaker are necessary;

23 and those members of the body which we deem less honorable, on these we bestow more abundant honor, and our less presentable members become much more presentable,

24 whereas our more presentable members have no need of it.

1 CORINTHIANS 12:24B–27

24 But God has so composed the body, giving more abundant honor to that member which lacked,

25 so that there may be no division in the body, but that the members may have the same care for one another.

26 And if one member suffers, all the members suffer with it; if one member is honored, all the members rejoice with it.

27 Now you are Christ's body, and individually members of it.

OBSERVE

Leader: Read 1 Corinthians 12:24b–27 aloud. Have the group say and…
- *draw a stick figure over each occurrence of the word **body**.*
- *circle each reference to **member(s)**.*

DISCUSS
- What do verses 24–25 identify as a problem God wants us to avoid?

- How are the members to relate to one another?

- What do we learn about believers in verse 27?

OBSERVE

Leader: Read 1 Corinthians 12:29–30.

• *Have the group say aloud and mark each occurrence of the word **all** with a big **A.***

DISCUSS

• Does everyone have the same gift?

• Do all members have all of the gifts?

29 All are not apostles, are they? All are not prophets, are they? All are not teachers, are they? All are not workers of miracles, are they?

30 All do not have gifts of healings, do they? All do not speak with tongues, do they? All do not interpret, do they?

ROMANS 12:3–6

3 For through the grace given to me I say to everyone among you not to think more highly of himself than he ought to think; but to think so as to have sound judgment, as God has allotted to each a measure of faith.

4 For just as we have many members in one body and all the members do not have the same function,

5 so we, who are many, are one body in Christ, and individually members one of another.

6 Since we have gifts that differ according to

OBSERVE

As we've already seen, in his letter to believers in local churches in Rome, Paul made a clear connection between our surrender to God and how we exercise our spiritual gifts. Let's look again at that passage to see how our surrender impacts our interactions with one another.

Leader: Read Romans 12:3–6 aloud. Have the group…
- *circle each reference to **members**.*
- *draw a stick figure over every occurrence of the word **body**.*

DISCUSS

- How does the message in verse 3 relate to what Paul is saying in verses 4–6?

- What did you learn from marking *members*?

- How are the members to view their role within the body?

• Verse 6 restates what we've seen: each believer has a different gift. Do you know your spiritual gift? Explain your answer.

the grace given to us, each of us is to exercise them accordingly.

• How are you to be using it in the body? In other words, what is your area of service?

• How are you using your gift to benefit the body?

OBSERVE

Let's look at a passage in which Paul describes what happens when differently gifted members of the body function as intended, equipping the saints and serving the Lord and others.

Leader: *Read Ephesians 4:14–16 aloud. Have the group say and...*
- *mark every reference to **Christ**, including pronouns, with a cross:* ✝
- *draw a stick figure over each occurrence of the word **body**.*

EPHESIANS 4:14–16

14 As a result, we are no longer to be children, tossed here and there by waves and carried about by every wind of doctrine, by the trickery of men, by craftiness in deceitful scheming;

15 but speaking the truth in love, we are to

grow up in all aspects into Him who is the head, even Christ,

16 from whom the whole body, being fitted and held together by what every joint supplies, according to the proper working of each individual part, causes the growth of the body for the building up of itself in love.

DISCUSS

• What did you learn from marking *body*?

• What causes growth—an increase in strength and health—in the body of Christ?

• What does Paul mean by the term "grow up" in verse 15?

• Can a hand do the rest of the body any good if it is severed?

• How does this relate to the need of every believer to participate in the life of the church?

• Discuss how the hidden parts of your physical body affect the function of the more obvious parts, like your feet and hands. What does this suggest about those who work behind the scenes in the life of the church?

• How would your church be impacted if believers knew what their gifts were and used them to equip the body, to serve God and others?

• Are you connected to the body of Christ through active participation in your local church? If not—if you're severed from the body—what is the effect on you, based on what you've read here? On the church?

• If you are connected to a local church, in what ways are you contributing to the health and growth of the body?

• What are some additional ways you sense God directing you to use your gifts to build up His church in love?

WRAP IT UP

For the church to be healthy, like a strong body, we first of all need to realize that *we need one another*. There's no such thing as a spiritually vibrant Lone Ranger Christian. God designed us to function best when we are working together. Yet far too often people become so engrossed in their own bit of the ministry, and so convinced of its supreme importance, that they neglect or even criticize others who have different gifts or ministries. Others decide that the church doesn't need their "small" contribution, so they decline to participate. But in truth, *all* of us—all our spiritual gifts, all our ministries, all the results that God brings through us—are needed for the body to be healthy and whole.

A second sign of a healthy church is that *we respect one another*. The hidden parts of your body—your tendons and ligaments, your organs and blood vessels—are absolutely vital to your ability to think and breathe and move. So too with the church, all members contribute in vital ways to the overall work of God, even when the results may be unclear. All service ranks the same with God. Whenever we get caught up in focusing on our own importance—or worrying about our lack of significance—in the church, we cease to bring glory to God and strength to the body.

Third, for a church to truly thrive it's vital that *we sympathize with one another*. If any one part of the body is affected, all the others suffer in sympathy because they cannot help it. The church is a whole. The person who cannot see beyond his or her own organization, the person who cannot see beyond his or her congregation—worse still, the person who cannot see beyond his or her own family circle—has not even begun to grasp the blessing that comes through the genuine unity of the church.

Are you in position to be effective and to function within the body as God intends? If not, we urge you to find a local church and ask God to show you how to exercise your spiritual gifts for building up the body in love.

As a Christian you have a spiritual gift! Have you let that truth grip your heart? You, right where you are as you complete this study, have a spiritual gift. You didn't choose it—that is the responsibility of the Holy Spirit—but you do have one. The God who created the heavens and the earth has chosen to make His Spirit resident in your life.

He doesn't need us, but He has chosen to gift us to accomplish the work of His kingdom. In a sense He lets us co-labor with Him by operating in our area of giftedness. This truth should set your heart on fire to worship Him, to praise Him, and to serve Him by serving His Son's bride, the church.

In this last lesson we will look at a few examples of spiritual gifts at work in the lives of New Testament believers. It is not always obvious exactly what their gifts are, but we will see the impact that results from being surrendered to God.

OBSERVE

Because of persecution, believers in the early church were scattered. As they moved, the word of God spread with them. Among the scattered Jews was Philip, an apostle who went to the Samaritans, a people group including both Jews and Gentiles. Up until this point the apostles had not gone to Samaria.

Acts 8:4–5, 12; 21:8

4 Therefore, those who had been scattered went about preaching the word.

5 Philip went down to the city of Samaria and began proclaiming Christ to them.

12 But when they believed Philip preaching the good news about the kingdom of God and the name of Jesus Christ, they were being baptized, men and women alike.

21:8 On the next day we left and came to Caesarea, and entering the house of Philip the evangelist, who was one of the seven, we stayed with him.

Leader: Read Acts 8:4–5, 12; and 21:8 aloud.

• Have the group say and mark every reference to Philip, including pronouns, with a big P.

DISCUSS

• What did you learn from marking the references to Philip?

INSIGHT

The Greek word translated as *preaching* in Acts 8:4 means to "preach the gospel, to evangelize."

• We learned in earlier lessons that God gives ministries in relation to gifts. With that in mind, what would you identify as Philip's spiritual gift(s)?

• What does Philip's story reveal about how the gift(s) he had are intended to help the church?

OBSERVE

As we've seen, every believer receives gifts from the Holy Spirit. So let's look at some of the less-prominent believers in the early church to see how they used theirs.

Leader: Read Acts 18:24–28 aloud. Have the group…
- *circle every reference to **Apollos,** including pronouns and the phrase **this man.***
- *underline the phrase **explained to him the way of God more accurately.***

DISCUSS

- What did you learn about Apollos from this passage?

- What gift(s) did he appear to have?

- Who *explained the way of God more accurately* to him?

- What spiritual gift(s) might have equipped Priscilla and/or Aquila to accurately explain the Scriptures?

ACTS 18:24–28

24 Now a Jew named Apollos, an Alexandrian by birth, an eloquent man, came to Ephesus; and he was mighty in the Scriptures.

25 This man had been instructed in the way of the Lord; and being fervent in spirit, he was speaking and teaching accurately the things concerning Jesus, being acquainted only with the baptism of John;

26 and he began to speak out boldly in the synagogue. But when Priscilla and Aquila heard him, they took him aside and explained to him the way of God more accurately.

27 And when he wanted to go across to Achaia, the brethren encouraged him and wrote to the disciples to welcome him; and when he had arrived, he greatly helped those who had believed through grace,

28 for he powerfully refuted the Jews in public, demonstrating by the Scriptures that Jesus was the Christ.

• Do you think you may have the gift of teaching? If so, explain why you believe this is your gift.

• If you are not sure, ask yourself the following questions:

Do I feel drawn to and passionate about studying Scripture?

When I am given the opportunity to teach, do I feel comfortable doing so?

Do I sense that others are positively affected by my teaching?

What do others, not just my friends, say about my teaching?

OBSERVE

The early church was unified not only spiritually but also materially. They considered all things as common property. Because of their generosity, there was not a needy person among them. However, one couple in the church merely pretended to be generous rather than truly giving from their hearts. Let's see what happened.

Leader: Read Acts 5:1–6 aloud. Have the group...

• *mark every reference to **Peter** with a* **P.**
• *draw a cloud shape like this* ☁ *around **the Holy Spirit.***

DISCUSS

• What spiritual gift might Peter have been exercising here in recognizing the deception of Ananias? (Feel free to look back at the list on page 39 if you need help.)

ACTS 5:1–6

¹ But a man named Ananias, with his wife Sapphira, sold a piece of property,

² and kept back some of the price for himself, with his wife's full knowledge, and bringing a portion of it, he laid it at the apostles' feet.

³ But Peter said, "Ananias, why has Satan filled your heart to lie to the Holy Spirit and to keep back some of the price of the land?

⁴ "While it remained unsold, did it not remain your own? And after it was sold, was it not under your control? Why is

it that you have conceived this deed in your heart? You have not lied to men but to God."

5 And as he heard these words, Ananias fell down and breathed his last; and great fear came over all who heard of it.

6 The young men got up and covered him up, and after carrying him out, they buried him.

• According to verse 5, what effect did this incident have on the church?

• Discuss why the exercise of this gift is vital to the body of Christ.

OBSERVE

This next passage describes the beginning of Paul's first missionary journey. (Saul's name is later changed to Paul.) It is interesting to see how the church was described and how they understood the calling of Paul.

You may notice that sometimes in Scripture it is hard to tell whether a passage refers to gifts, or to ministries, or to both. This is one of those passages.

Leader: Read Acts 13:1–5 aloud. Have the group say and…
- *draw a box around each of **the gifts** mentioned.*
- *draw a cloud shape around each mention of **the Holy Spirit,** including pronouns.*

DISCUSS

- According to verse 1, what institution was the Holy Spirit working through?

ACTS 13:1–5

¹ Now there were at Antioch, in the church that was there, prophets and teachers: Barnabas, and Simeon who was called Niger, and Lucius of Cyrene, and Manaen who had been brought up with Herod the tetrarch, and Saul.

² While they were ministering to the Lord and fasting, the Holy Spirit said, "Set apart for Me Barnabas and Saul for the work to which I have called them."

³ Then, when they had fasted and prayed and laid their hands on them, they sent them away.

4 So, being sent out by the Holy Spirit, they went down to Seleucia and from there they sailed to Cyprus.

5 When they reached Salamis, they began to proclaim the word of God in the synagogues of the Jews; and they also had John as their helper.

• What gifts or ministries did you see mentioned in these verses?

• What did you learn from marking reference to the Holy Spirit?

INSIGHT

The action described in the phrase *placed their hands on* identified the church with the ministry of these men and acknowledged God's direction for them.

• How does this relate to what you've learned about spiritual gifts?

• Who in this passage gives the ministry?

• Why do you believe Barnabas and Saul had John with them as their helper? Discuss what they might have seen in his life that compelled them to bring him along.

• One way of identifying your own spiritual gift(s) is asking others. Often others see your area of giftedness before you do. What kinds of things do others ask you to do?

• What kind of activities, attitudes, or behavior do others compliment you on?

• What spiritual gift(s) might this point to and why?

ACTS 3:1–10

1 Now Peter and John were going up to the temple at the ninth hour, the hour of prayer.

2 And a man who had been lame from his mother's womb was being carried along, whom they used to set down every day at the gate of the temple which is called Beautiful, in order to beg alms of those who were entering the temple.

3 When he saw Peter and John about to go into the temple, he began asking to receive alms.

4 But Peter, along with John, fixed his gaze on him and said, "Look at us!"

OBSERVE

Shortly after the outpouring of the Holy Spirit at Pentecost, two of the disciples were traveling up to the temple in Jerusalem to pray.

Leader: Read Acts 3:1–10 aloud. Have the group...
- *mark every reference to **Peter,** including pronouns, with a **P.***
- *circle every reference to **the lame man,** including pronouns.*

DISCUSS

- What did you learn from marking the references to the lame man?

- How did Peter respond to the man's request for alms? Did he give him some?

• What did Peter do?

5 And he began to give them his attention, expecting to receive something from them.

• What spiritual gift did Peter exhibit through this action?

6 But Peter said, "I do not possess silver and gold, but what I do have I give to you: In the name of Jesus Christ the Nazarene—walk!"

• Who enabled him to do this? Explain your answer from the text.

7 And seizing him by the right hand, he raised him up; and immediately his feet and his ankles were strengthened.

• How did the man respond to his healing?

8 With a leap he stood upright and began to walk; and he entered the temple with them, walking and leaping and praising God.

• Who did he acknowledge as the one who healed him? Why is that important?

9 And all the people saw him walking and praising God;

10 and they were taking note of him as being the one who used to sit at the Beautiful Gate of the temple to beg alms, and they were filled with wonder and amazement at what had happened to him.

• How did the people respond?

• Throughout the Scriptures we see this repeated phrase: *that they may know that I am God.* How would that phrase relate to the purpose of this gift in the church?

ROMANS 16:1–2

1 I commend to you our sister Phoebe, who is a servant of the church which is at Cenchrea;

2 that you receive her in the Lord in a

OBSERVE

In his closing remarks to the church in the city of Rome, Paul mentioned Phoebe, a servant of the church.

Leader: *Read Romans 16:1–2 aloud.*
  • *Have the group circle each mention of* ***Phoebe,*** *including pronouns.*

DISCUSS

• What gift does this passage say Phoebe had?

• How did she exercise her gift?

• What would the gift of service look like in action today?

• Do you have the gift of service? Explain your answer.

• Do you tend to notice a need before anyone else does?

manner worthy of the saints, and that you help her in whatever matter she may have need of you; for she herself has also been a helper of many, and of myself as well.

WRAP IT UP

While this course is not designed to tell you exactly what your spiritual gift is, we wanted to close the study with some questions that might help you find your place of service in the body of Christ.[*]

When it comes to knowing what your gift is, the first place to start is in prayer. After all, your gift comes from the Holy Spirit; ask Him which one He gave you. After prayer, think through the following questions, designed to help you determine whether your area of giftedness is speaking or serving, and possibly even what your specific spiritual gift(s) may be:

- Do you ever volunteer for any type of job or service to others? If so, what? Why that particular job?
- Do you feel drawn to address a particular need or to interact with a particular type of people? If so, what is it? Why do you find this so compelling?
- What are the strongest areas of your Christian life? What are the weakest areas of your Christian life?
- If you had a choice been two jobs in the church—one requiring a lot of verbal communication in one form or another and the other requiring you simply to perform a task—which job would you prefer, and why?

In addition to prayerfully asking God and examining your own life when it comes to spiritual gifts, you should involve others in your

---

[*] If you're looking for an in-depth study of spiritual gifts, you may want to consider the Precept Upon Precept workbook *Spiritual Gifts,* available at www.precept.org.

search, particularly those who are spiritually mature and know you well. They may have some helpful insights that lead in unexpected directions.

Once you think you've identified your spiritual gift(s), ask God where He wants you to serve in the body of Christ. Even if you aren't certain, jump in and try something out. When you are working in an area of ministry in the church that fits your gift, it will probably feel like a good fit. Most likely it will feel natural, comfortable.

Whatever you do, don't waste the gift God has given you. Remember, He has designed the body to need each member. When each member works together as intended, the church functions properly and together we are a light shining in the darkness.

So pray, seek, and ask the Holy Spirit to help you find your gift and your area of service. Without you the church is handicapped.

Then get to work in the body of Christ.

4⦿ MINUTE BIBLE STUDIES

No-Homework
That Help You

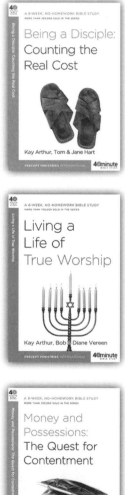

A 6-WEEK, NO-HOMEWORK BIBLE STUDY
MORE THAN 700,000 SOLD IN THE SERIES

Being a Disciple: Counting the Real Cost

Kay Arthur, Tom & Jane Hart

PRECEPT MINISTRIES INTERNATIONAL · 4⦿minute BIBLE STUDY

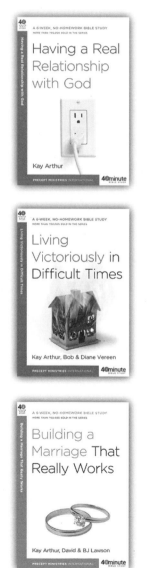

A 6-WEEK, NO-HOMEWORK BIBLE STUDY
MORE THAN 700,000 SOLD IN THE SERIES

Having a Real Relationship with God

Kay Arthur

PRECEPT MINISTRIES INTERNATIONAL · 4⦿minute BIBLE STUDY

A 6-WEEK, NO-HOMEWORK BIBLE STUDY
MORE THAN 700,000 SOLD IN THE SERIES

How Do You Walk the Walk You Talk?

Kay Arthur

PRECEPT MINISTRIES INTERNATIONAL · 4⦿minute BIBLE STUDY

A 6-WEEK, NO-HOMEWORK BIBLE STUDY
MORE THAN 700,000 SOLD IN THE SERIES

Living a Life of True Worship

Kay Arthur, Bob & Diane Vereen

PRECEPT MINISTRIES INTERNATIONAL · 4⦿minute BIBLE STUDY

A 6-WEEK, NO-HOMEWORK BIBLE STUDY
MORE THAN 700,000 SOLD IN THE SERIES

Living Victoriously in Difficult Times

Kay Arthur, Bob & Diane Vereen

PRECEPT MINISTRIES INTERNATIONAL · 4⦿minute BIBLE STUDY

A 6-WEEK, NO-HOMEWORK BIBLE STUDY
MORE THAN 700,000 SOLD IN THE SERIES

How to Make Choices You Won't Regret

Kay Arthur, David & BJ Lawson

PRECEPT MINISTRIES INTERNATIONAL · 4⦿minute BIBLE STUDY

A 6-WEEK, NO-HOMEWORK BIBLE STUDY
MORE THAN 700,000 SOLD IN THE SERIES

Money and Possessions: The Quest for Contentment

Kay Arthur & David Arthur

PRECEPT MINISTRIES INTERNATIONAL · 4⦿minute BIBLE STUDY

A 6-WEEK, NO-HOMEWORK BIBLE STUDY
MORE THAN 700,000 SOLD IN THE SERIES

Building a Marriage That Really Works

Kay Arthur, David & BJ Lawson

PRECEPT MINISTRIES INTERNATIONAL · 4⦿minute BIBLE STUDY

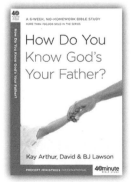

A 6-WEEK, NO-HOMEWORK BIBLE STUDY
MORE THAN 700,000 SOLD IN THE SERIES

How Do You Know God's Your Father?

Kay Arthur, David & BJ Lawson

PRECEPT MINISTRIES INTERNATIONAL · 4⦿minute BIBLE STUDY

Bible Studies
Discover Truth For Yourself

Also Available:
A Man's Strategy for Conquering Temptation
Rising to the Call of Leadership
Key Principles of Biblical Fasting
What Does the Bible Say About Sex?
Turning Your Heart Toward God
Fatal Distractions: Conquering Destructive Temptations
Spiritual Warfare: Overcoming the Enemy
The Power of Knowing God
Breaking Free from Fear

Another powerful study series
from beloved Bible teacher

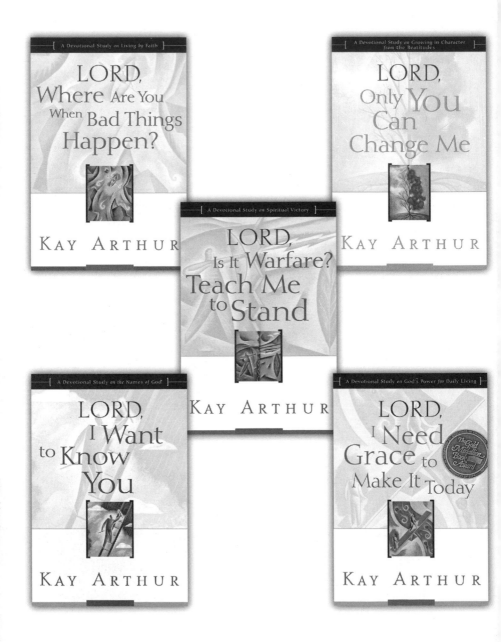

KAY ARTHUR

The Lord series provides insightful, warm-hearted Bible studies designed to meet you where you are—and help you discover God's answers to your deepest needs.

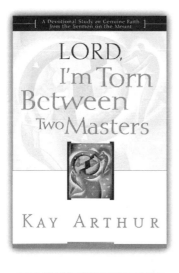

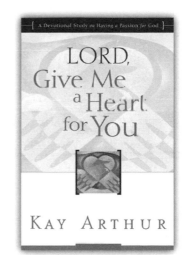

ALSO AVAILABLE:
One-year devotionals to draw you closer to the heart of God.

KAY ARTHUR is known around the world as an international Bible teacher, author, conference speaker, and host of the national radio and television programs *Precepts for Life*, which reaches a worldwide viewing audience of over 94 million. A four-time Gold Medallion Award–winning author, Kay has authored more than 100 books and Bible studies.

Kay and her husband, Jack, founded Precept Ministries International in 1970 in Chattanooga, Tennessee, with a vision to establish people in God's Word. Today, the ministry has a worldwide outreach. In addition to inductive study training workshops and thousands of small-group studies across America, PMI reaches nearly 150 countries with inductive Bible studies translated into nearly 70 languages, teaching people to discover Truth for themselves.

Contact Precept Ministries International for more information about inductive Bible studies in your area.

Precept Ministries International
P.O. Box 182218
Chattanooga, TN 37422-7218
800-763-8280
www.precept.org

ABOUT DAVID AND BJ LAWSON

DAVID AND BJ LAWSON have been involved with Precept Ministries International since 1980. After nine years in the pastorate, they joined PMI full-time as directors of the student ministries and staff teachers and trainers. A featured speaker at PMI conferences and in Precept Upon Precept videos, David writes for the Precept Upon Precept series, the New Inductive Study Series, and the 40-Minute Bible Studies series. BJ has written numerous 40-Minute Bible Studies and serves as the chief editor and developer of the series. In addition she is a featured speaker at PMI women's conferences.